ALL BUTTS ARE GOOD BUTTS

CELEBRATE YOUR DERRIERE

WITH

BOOTY AFFIRMATIONS,

AS*TROLOGY,

TUSHIE TRIVIA,

AND MORE!

RACHAL DUGGAN

ULYSSES PRESS

Published by:
ULYSSES PRESS
PO Box 3440
Berkeley, CA 94703
www.ulyssespress.com

ISBN: 978-1-64604-500-6

Printed in China
10 9 8 7 6 5 4 3 2 1

Cover design: Rachal Duggan

To my butt: You've had my back for so long.
You've inspired my career; you entertain me with your silly
sounds; and you shook my world when I was diagnosed with
irritable bowel syndrome (IBS) at age 13. You truly have a
thankless job. It feels only right to dedicate this book to you.
Thank you.

RAD

INTRODUCTION

When you think about it, butts have it all. They're practical, hilarious, iconic, and hardworking. Everyone has one and, yet, very few people are comfortable talking about it. Arguably the most predominant feature on our backside, each rump is like a fingerprint—unique and worthy of praise. But why do so many of us have such a complicated relationship with our buns? This book will examine all things booty, from historical legends to adorable animals to otherworldly asstrology. For those needing a little self-love, this book will cover fresh tactics to help you accept your perceived imperfections and easy strategies for honoring your cheeks. You'll laugh, you'll cry, and you'll (hopefully) see your glorious derriere in an entirely new light.

MAKING A CASE FOR BUTTS

Rumps need no introduction. And, in recent years, they are finally getting the attention they deserve. But here's a mini intro just for fun. Drumroll, please!

TICKLE
TICKLE

Z Z Z

SO COMFY...

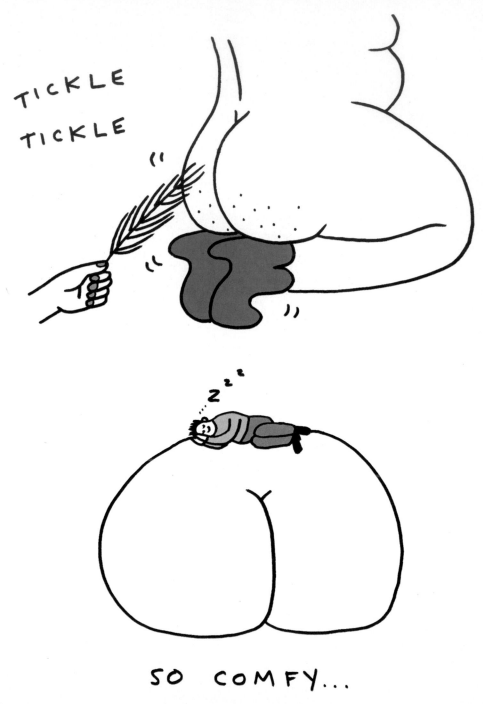

BUTTS ARE
FUN

ASK ANY ALIEN...

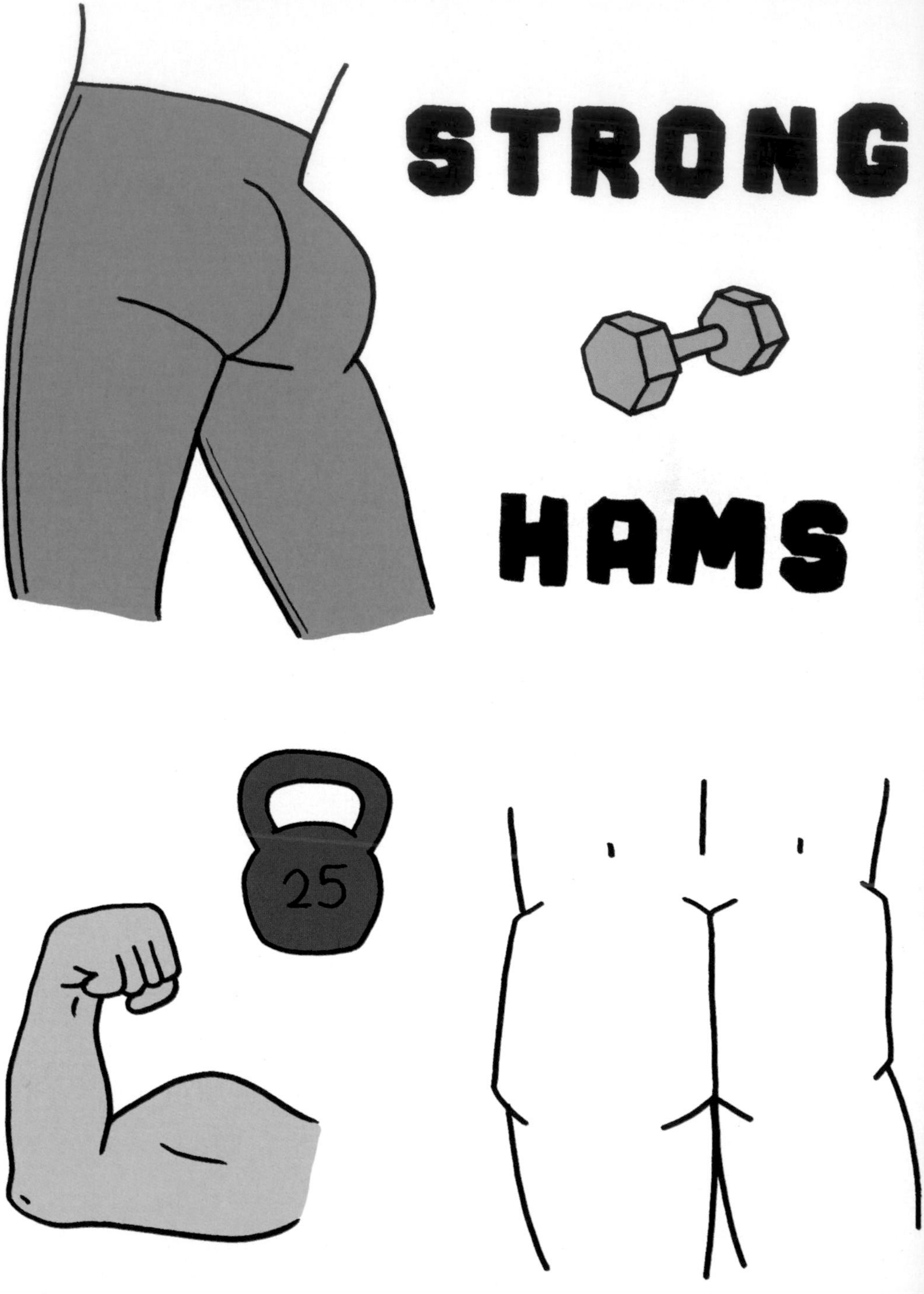
STRONG
HAMS
25

SMARTY PANTS
E=mc²

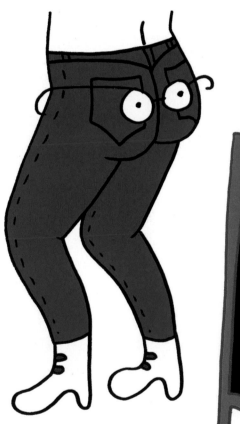

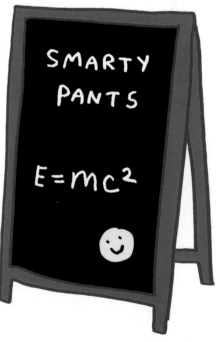

BUTTS ARE HUMBLE
AND PRACTICAL

Our butts are important af (as fuck) and rarely take a personal day. We take their "daily activities" for granted, but I would NOT want to experience life without one. The work they put in is less than glamorous and often goes unnoticed. Let's reflect on the thankless work they do for us.

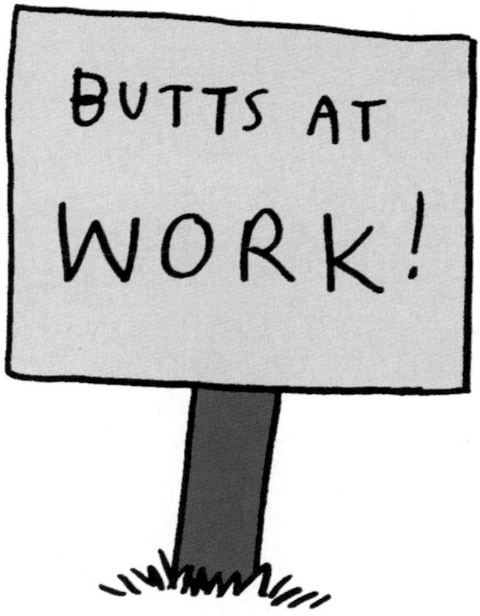
BUTTS AT
WORK!

TO DO:
POOP
FART 5-15 TIMES PER DAY
TO DO:
SIT
BE A CUSHION
BE STILL

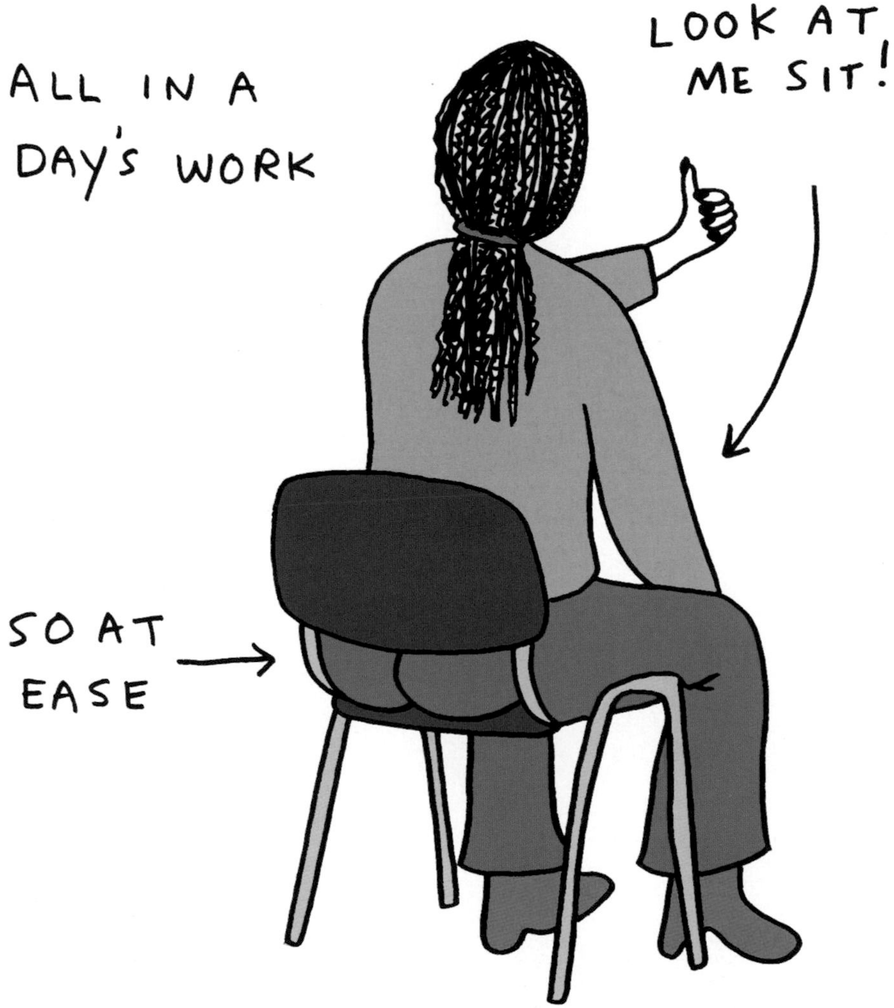
ALL IN A DAY'S WORK
LOOK AT ME SIT!
SO AT EASE

THE THRONE

WHERE THE REAL WORK HAPPENS

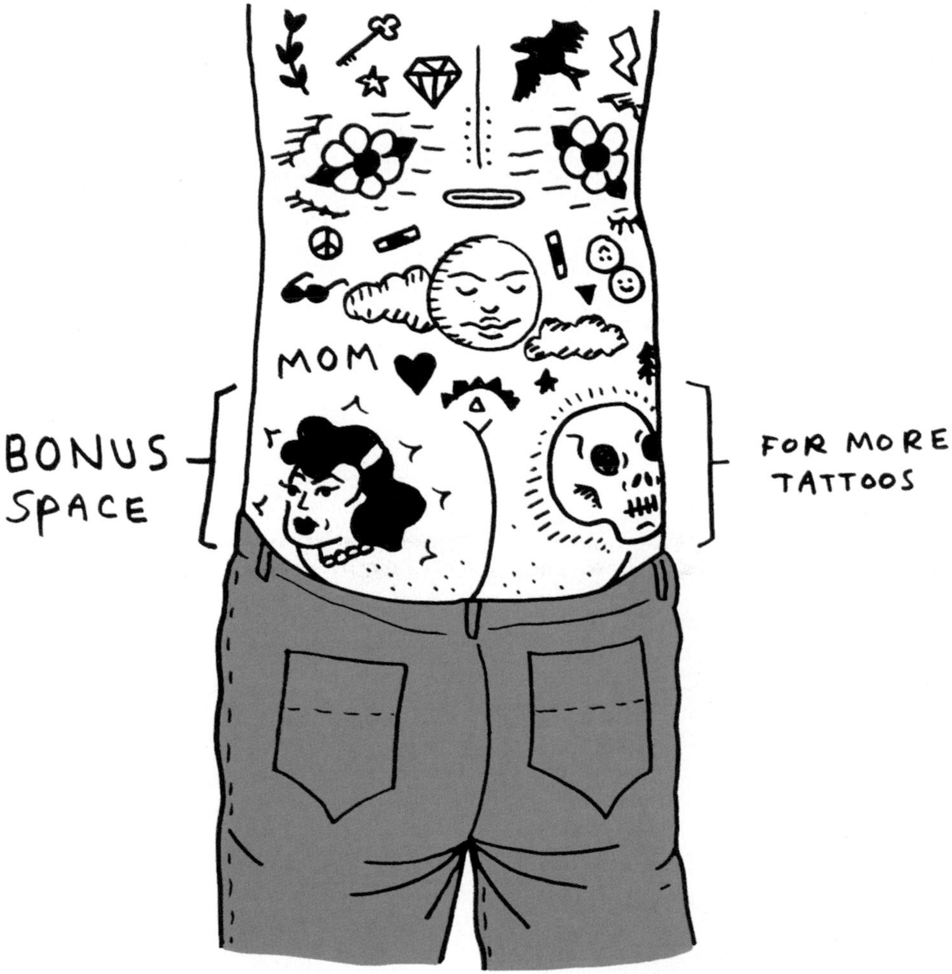
MOM
BONUS SPACE
FOR MORE TATTOOS

ICONIC BUTTS
THROUGH HISTORY

Let's take a stroll down booty memory lane, shall we? For every famous face, there's an equally iconic pair of cheeks worth highlighting. Please enjoy this very random, very star-studded assortment of famous butts.

FAMOUS BUTTS!

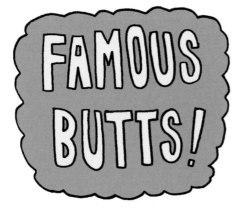

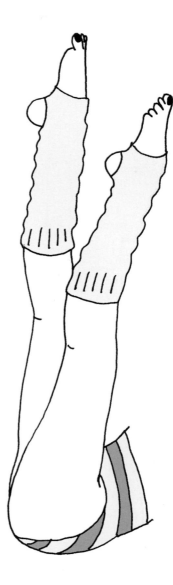

JANE FONDA

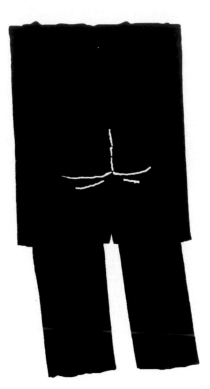

ABE LINCOLN

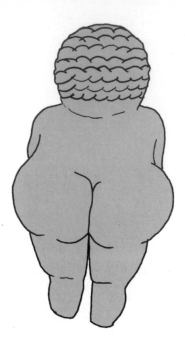

VENUS OF WILLENDORF

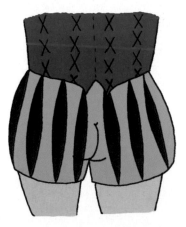

WILLIAM SHAKESPEARE

THE
DAVID

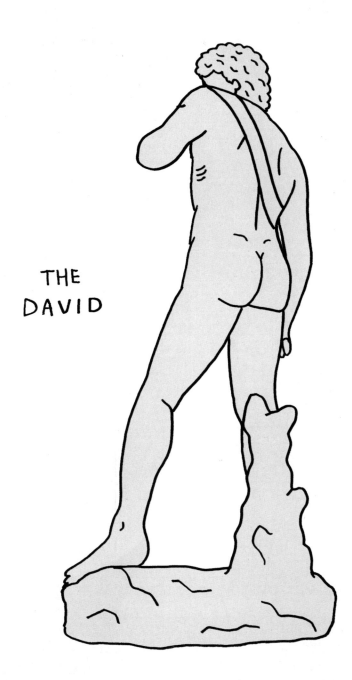

SHAKIRA

GEORGE MICHAEL

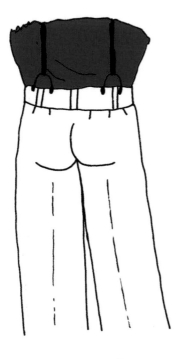

HARRY STYLES

LIZZO

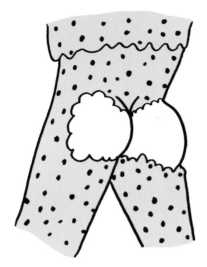

PRINCE

FREDDIE MERCURY

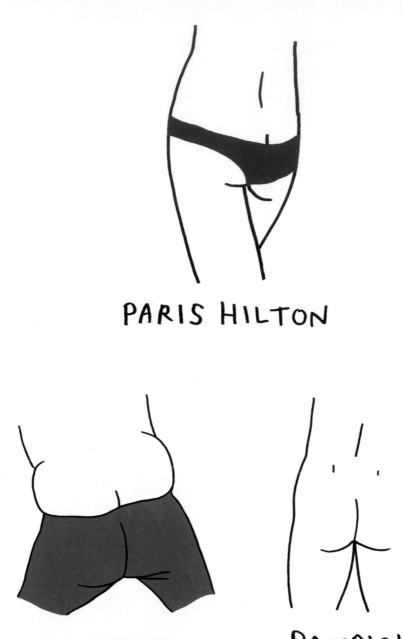

PARIS HILTON

CHRIS
FARLEY

PATRICK
SWAYZE

STIMPY

CARTOONS

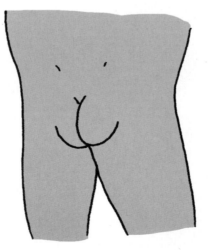

HANK HILL

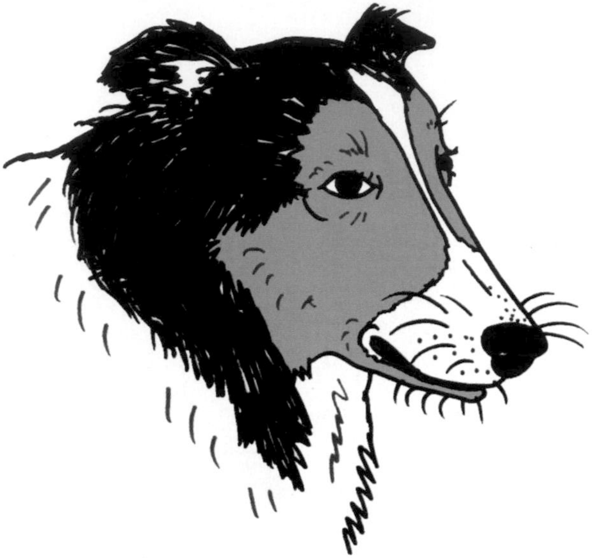

LASSIE

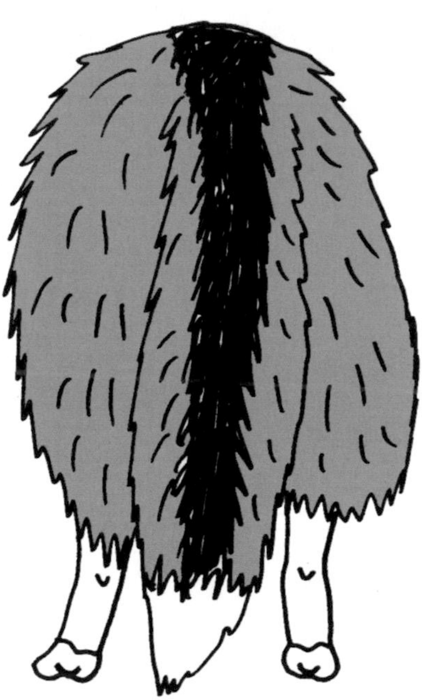

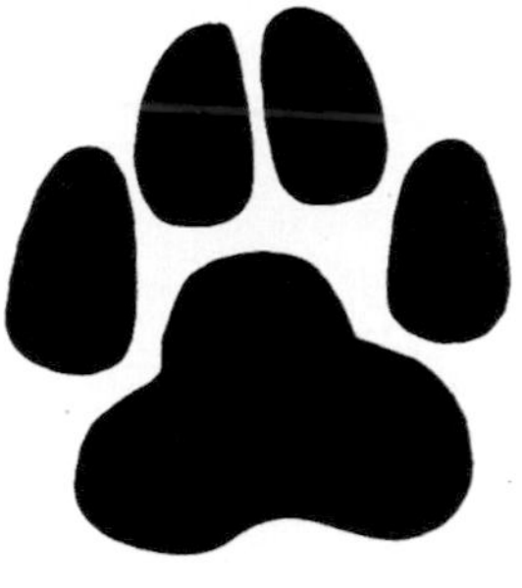

BUTT SHAME AND ACCEPTING YOUR BUTT

Life is too short to be at odds with your butt. What if we did the work to embrace what we had instead of fighting ourselves? It's much easier said than done, but accepting what you have can be so liberating. And who doesn't love a liberated fanny?!

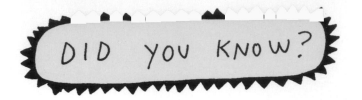

DID YOU KNOW?

BUTT ZITS HAPPEN.
AND THAT'S OK!

HIP DIPS
ARE NOT
A CAUSE
FOR
CONCERN

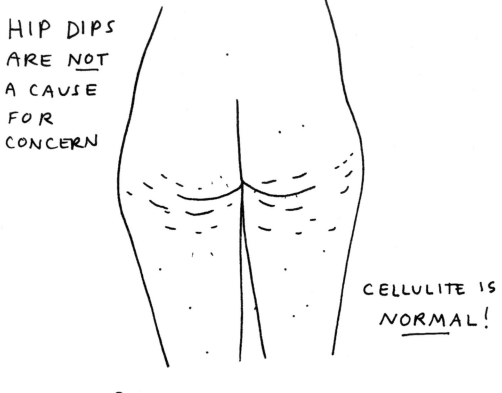

CELLULITE IS
NORMAL!

PEACH FUZZ
(PUN INTENDED)
IS CUTE

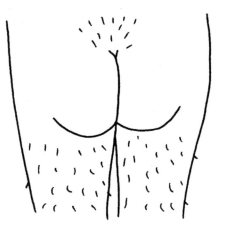

* YOUR BUTT IS
WORTHY OF LOVE

YOUR BUTT LOOKS GREAT!

* DON'T BE SO HARD
ON YOURSELF

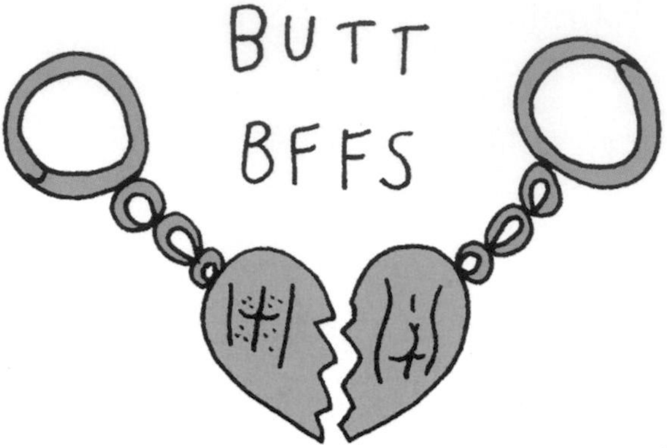
BUTT
BFFS

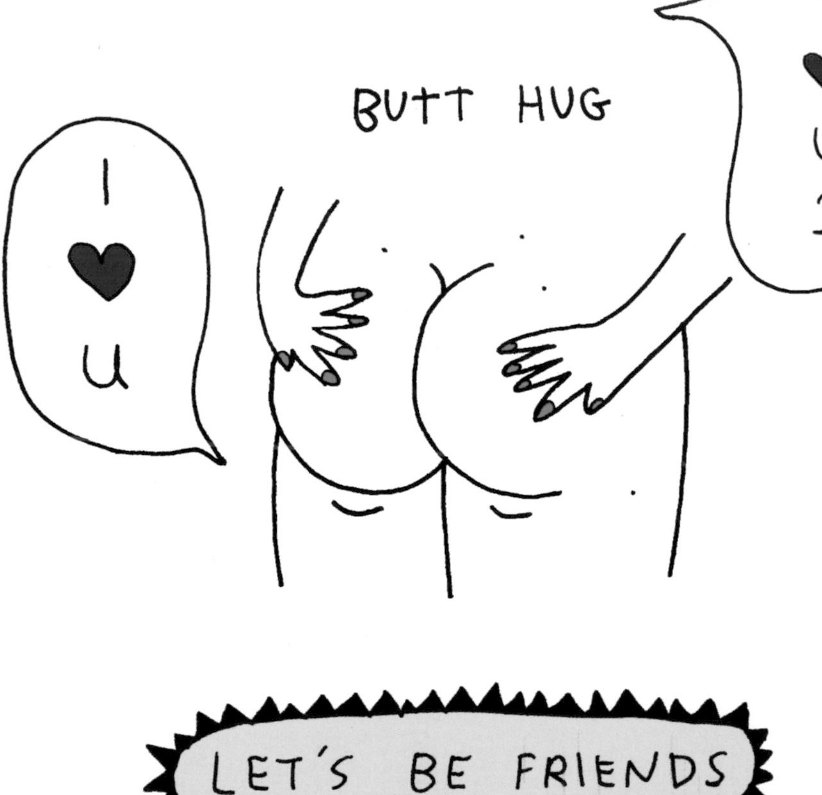
BUTT HUG
I ♥ U
I ♥ U 2

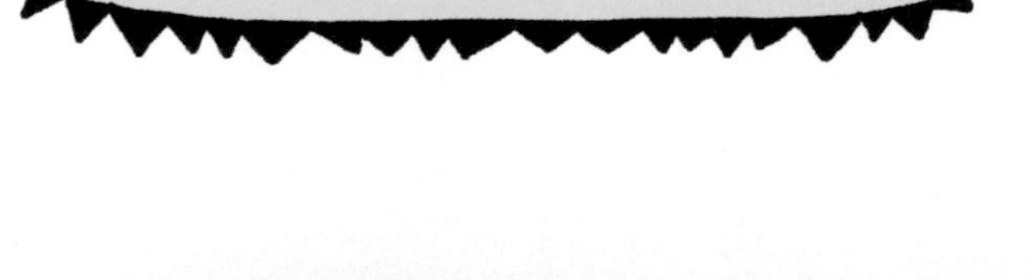
LET'S BE FRIENDS

MY BUTT IS

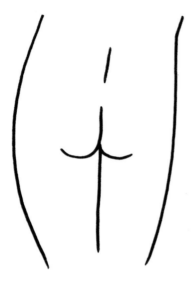

~~SO SMALL~~
GREAT AS
IT IS

MY BUTT
IS
~~LONG~~
MY BUTT

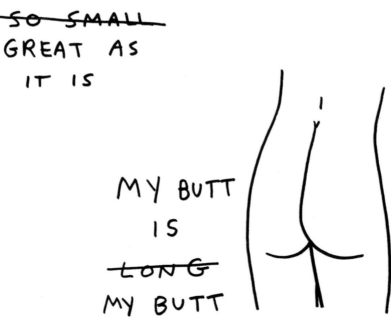

MY BUTT IS

~~TOO BIG~~

JUST RIGHT

BIG BUTTS ARE COOL

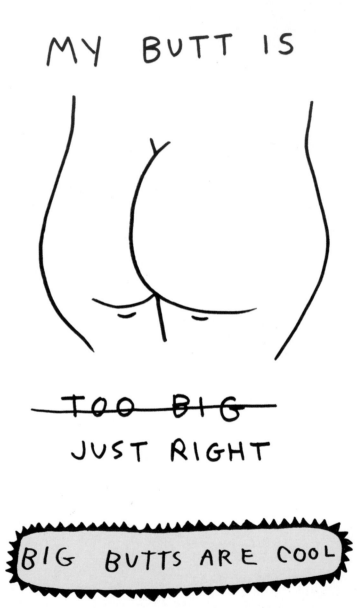

BUTTS ARE HILARIOUS

Have you heard one of those wild farts that could have stopped traffic? We all have. Some have the power to haunt you for life (aka blind date fart from hell) while others are just plain hilarious. If I had a dollar for every stinky toot, awkward grumble, and high-pitched butt-squeaks, I'd be rich!

LOL
FUNNY BUT STINKY AF

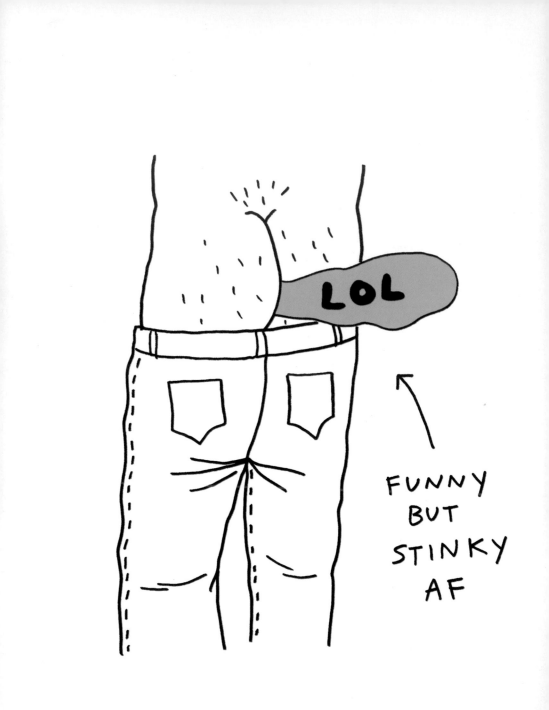

THE OG PRANKSTERS

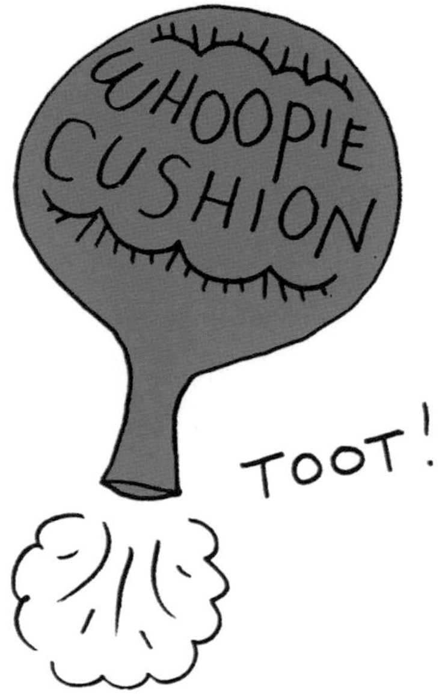
WHOOPIE CUSHION
TOOT!

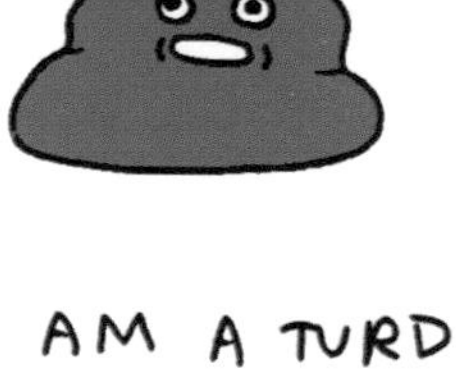

I AM A TURD

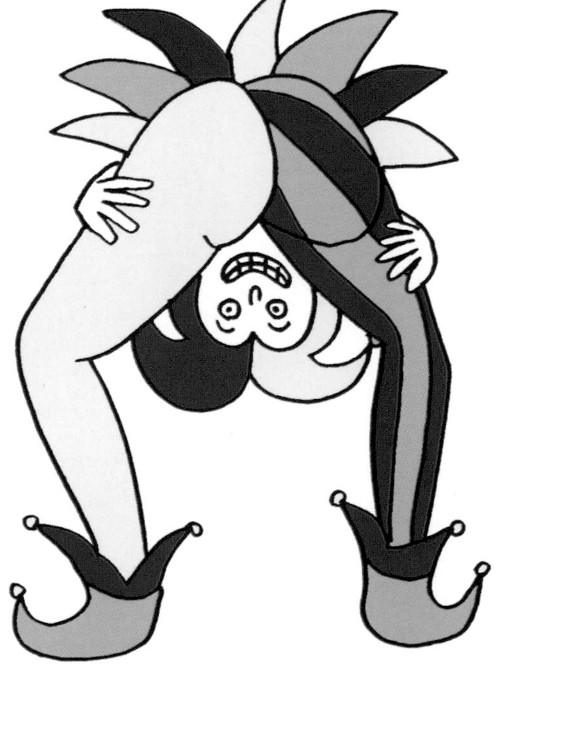

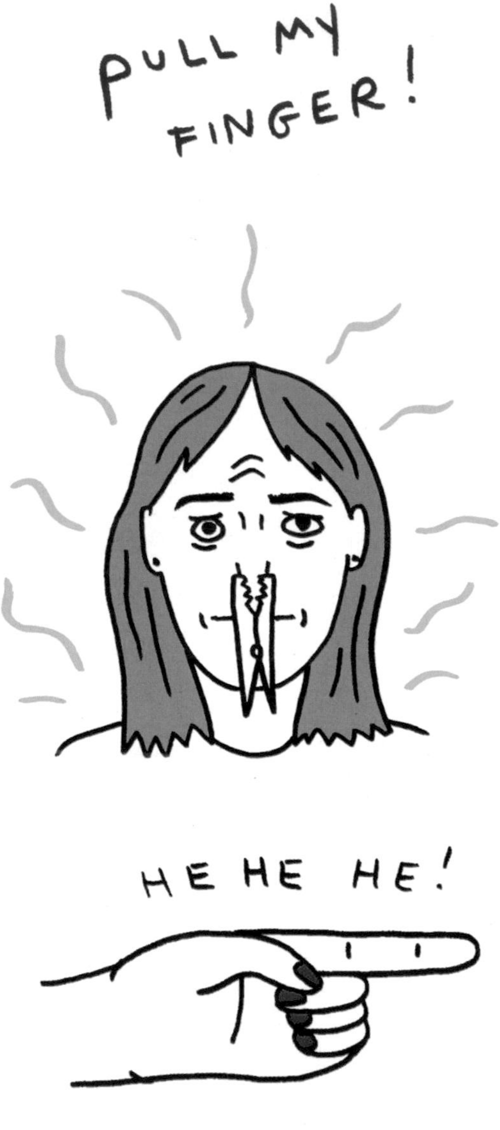
PULL MY FINGER!
HE HE HE!

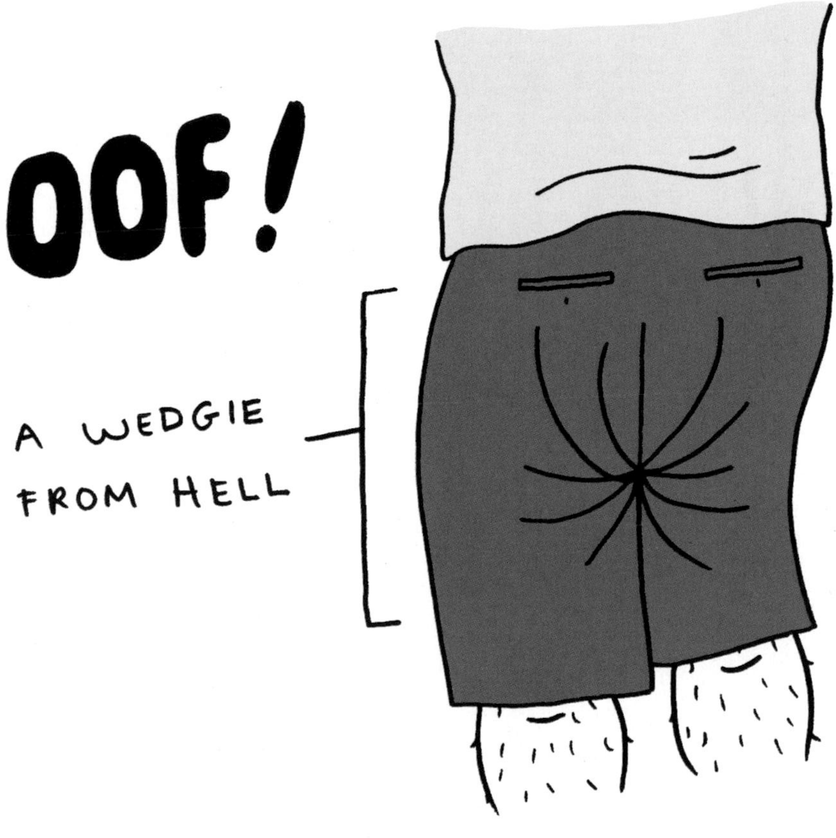
OOF!
A WEDGIE FROM HELL

ASSTROLOGY

Look to the stars for fascinating information about your rump! Who knew the heavens contained such specific wisdom? Your hindquarters will never be the same. Categorized by the four elements, here's your sign in cheeky form.

EARTH SIGNS

TAURUS

- INTELLIGENT
- DEPENDABLE
- STUBBORN

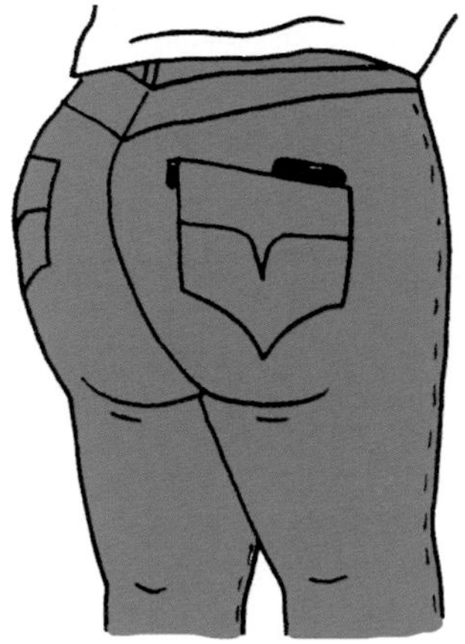

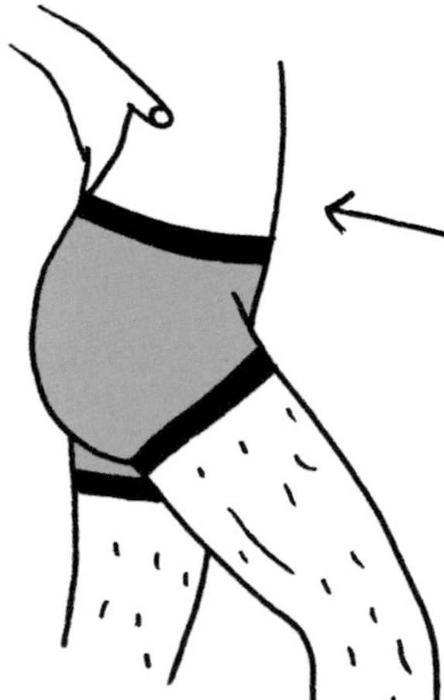

VIRGO

- SENSIBLE
- LOYAL
- PERFECTIONISTIC

CAPRICORN

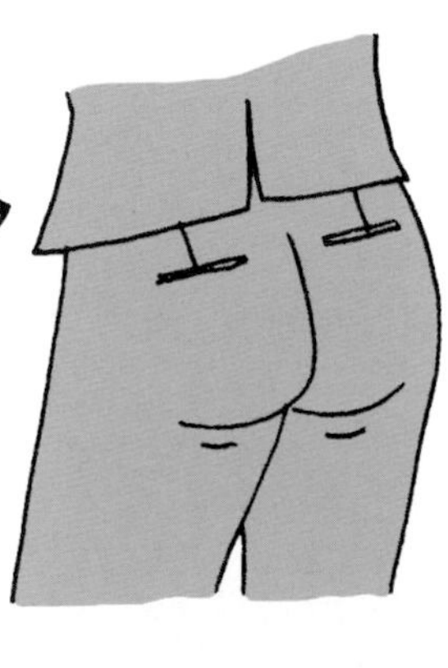

- AMBITIOUS
- DETERMINED
- STRICT

WATER SIGNS

CANCER

- EMOTIONAL
- DEVOTED
- PROTECTIVE

SCORPIO

- INDEPENDENT
- INTENSE
- SECRETIVE

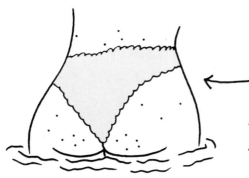

PISCES
- GRACIOUS
- SENSITIVE
- OPEN-MINDED

AIR SIGNS

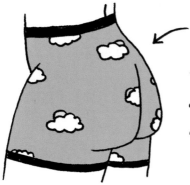

AQUARIUS

- INNOVATIVE
- CLEVER
- PROGRESSIVE

GEMINI

- EXTROVERTED
- PLAYFUL
- CHATTY AF

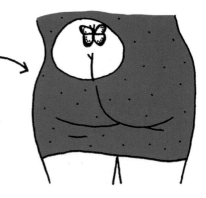

LIBRA

- PEACE KEEPER
- IDEALISTIC
- WELL-BALANCED

FIRE SIGNS

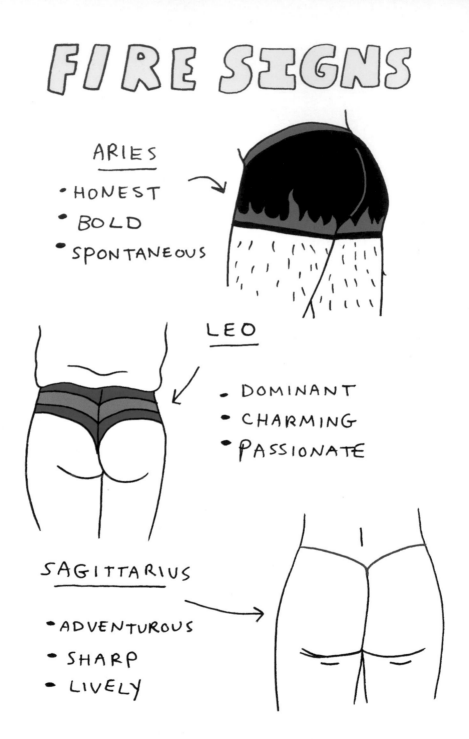

ARIES

- HONEST
- BOLD
- SPONTANEOUS

LEO

- DOMINANT
- CHARMING
- PASSIONATE

SAGITTARIUS

- ADVENTUROUS
- SHARP
- LIVELY

OMG, ANIMAL BUNS ARE CUTE

~~~ ☆ ▽ ◠◠ ☮ ♡

Hold on to your butts (or your hats)! The cuteness overload you are about to see requires a warning. Please give yourself a moment to fully appreciate these absolutely *freaking* adorable animal tushies. I can't even.

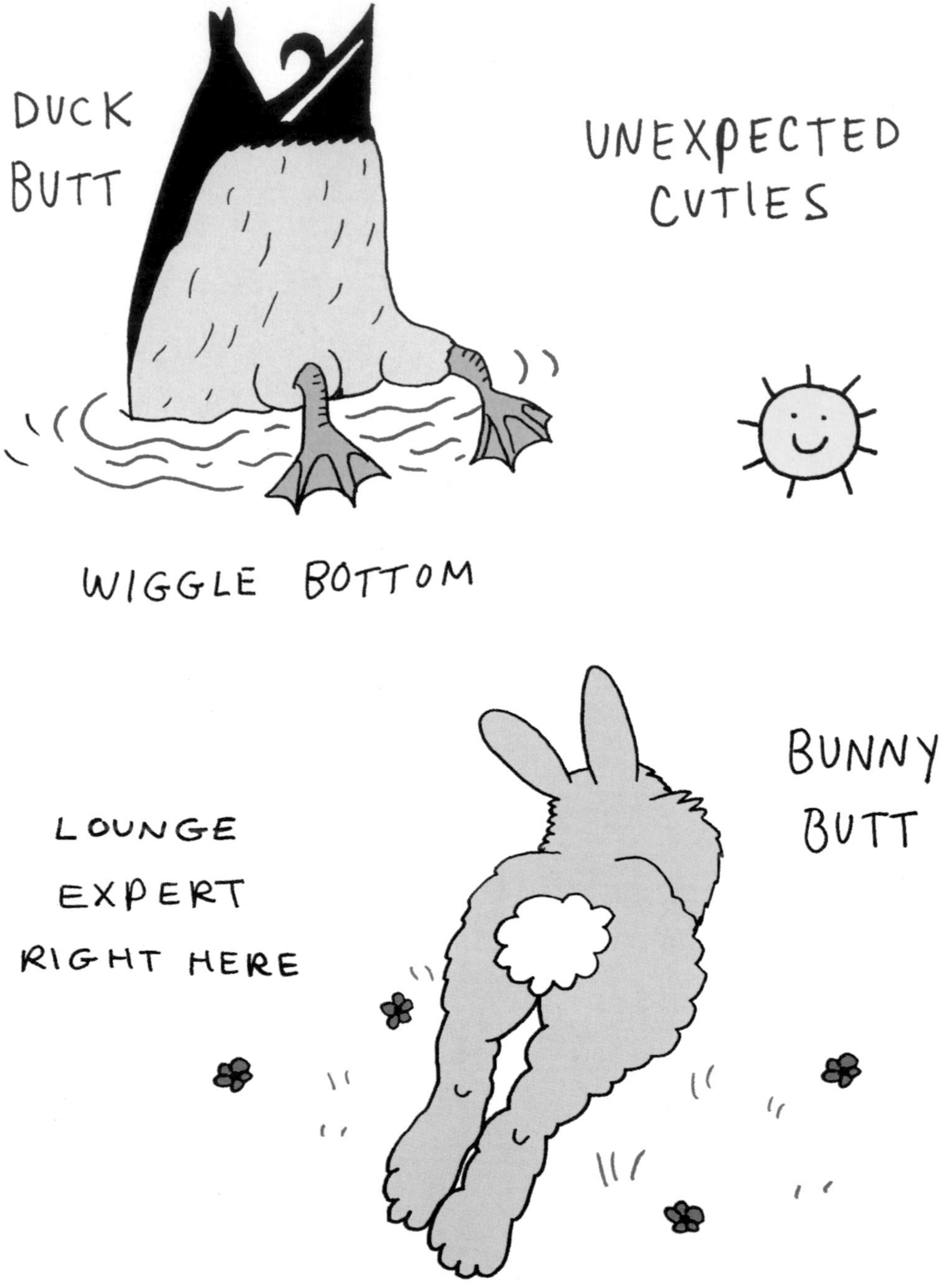
DUCK BUTT
UNEXPECTED CUTIES
WIGGLE BOTTOM
BUNNY BUTT
LOUNGE EXPERT RIGHT HERE

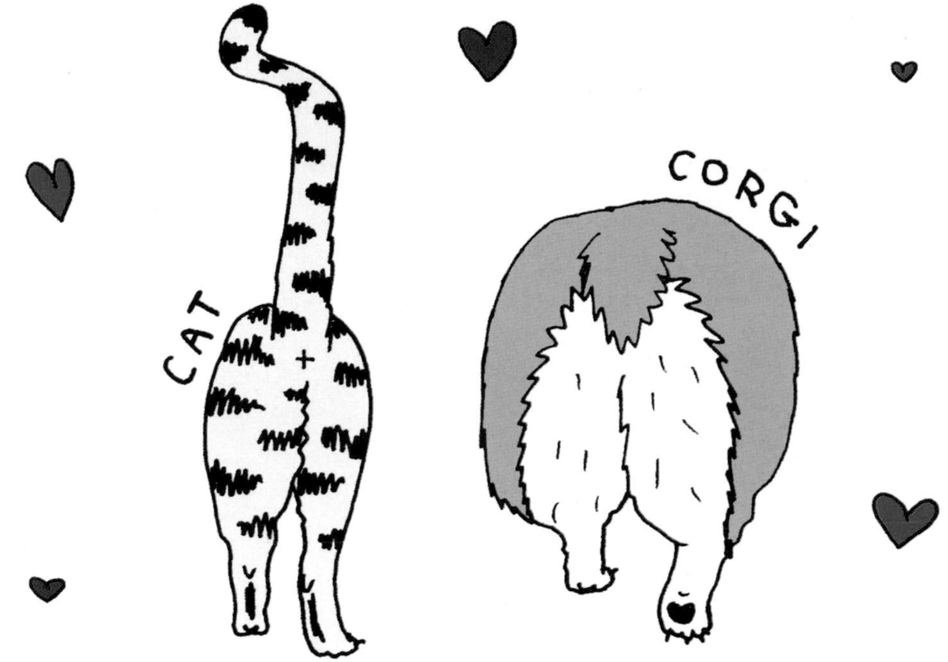
CAT
CORGI

FAMILIAR FAVORITES

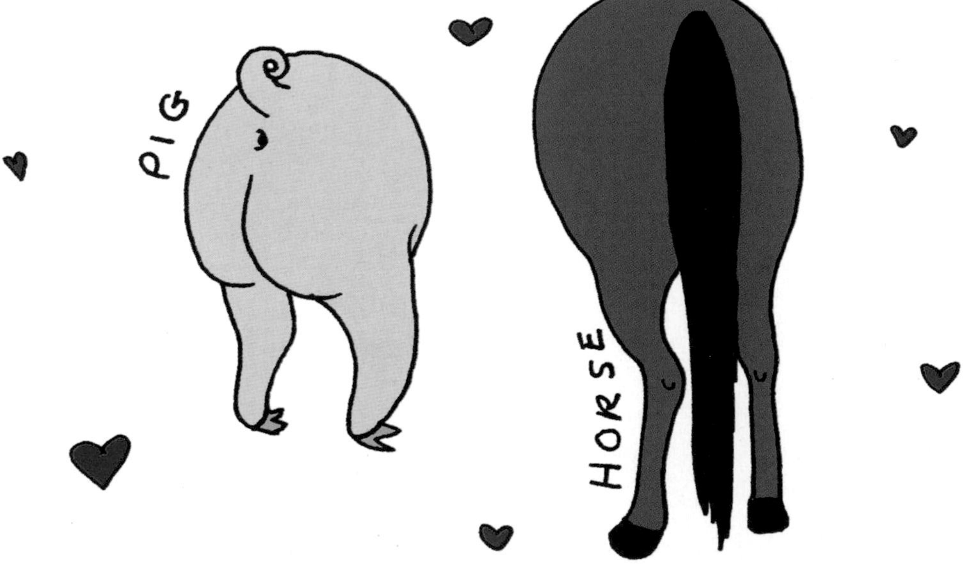
PIG
HORSE

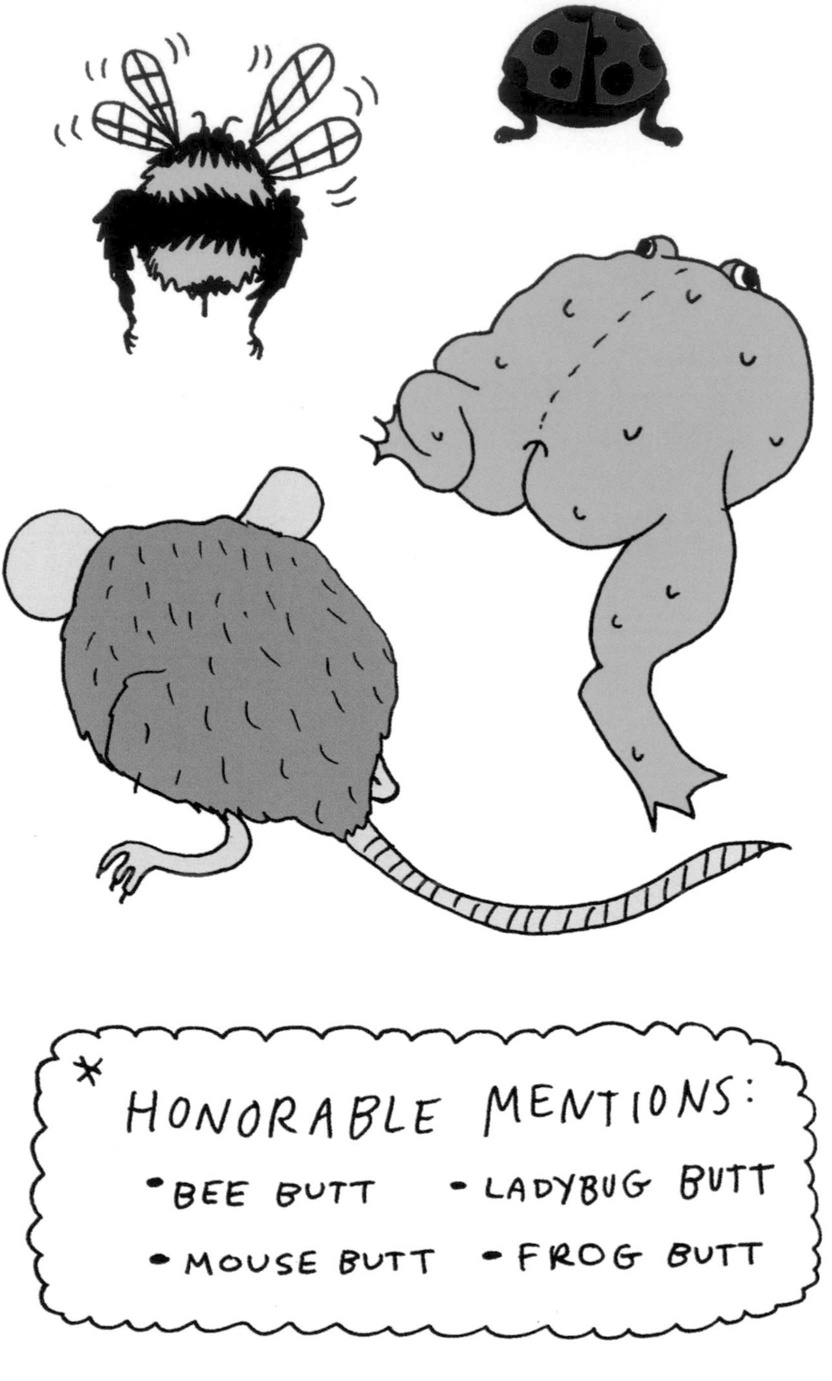

* HONORABLE MENTIONS:

- BEE BUTT
- LADYBUG BUTT
- MOUSE BUTT
- FROG BUTT

JUST FOR **FUN**

TO DO: LOOK UP STARFISH BUTT ONLINE.

BOOTY SELF-CARE (WHAT BUTTS WANT)

The gluteus maximus golden rule: do not neglect! Keisters have needs, just like you and me. A little TLC (tender loving care), some pampering, and attention. Let's go over the basics to make sure we're all taking excellent care of our butts. They deserve it and so do you.

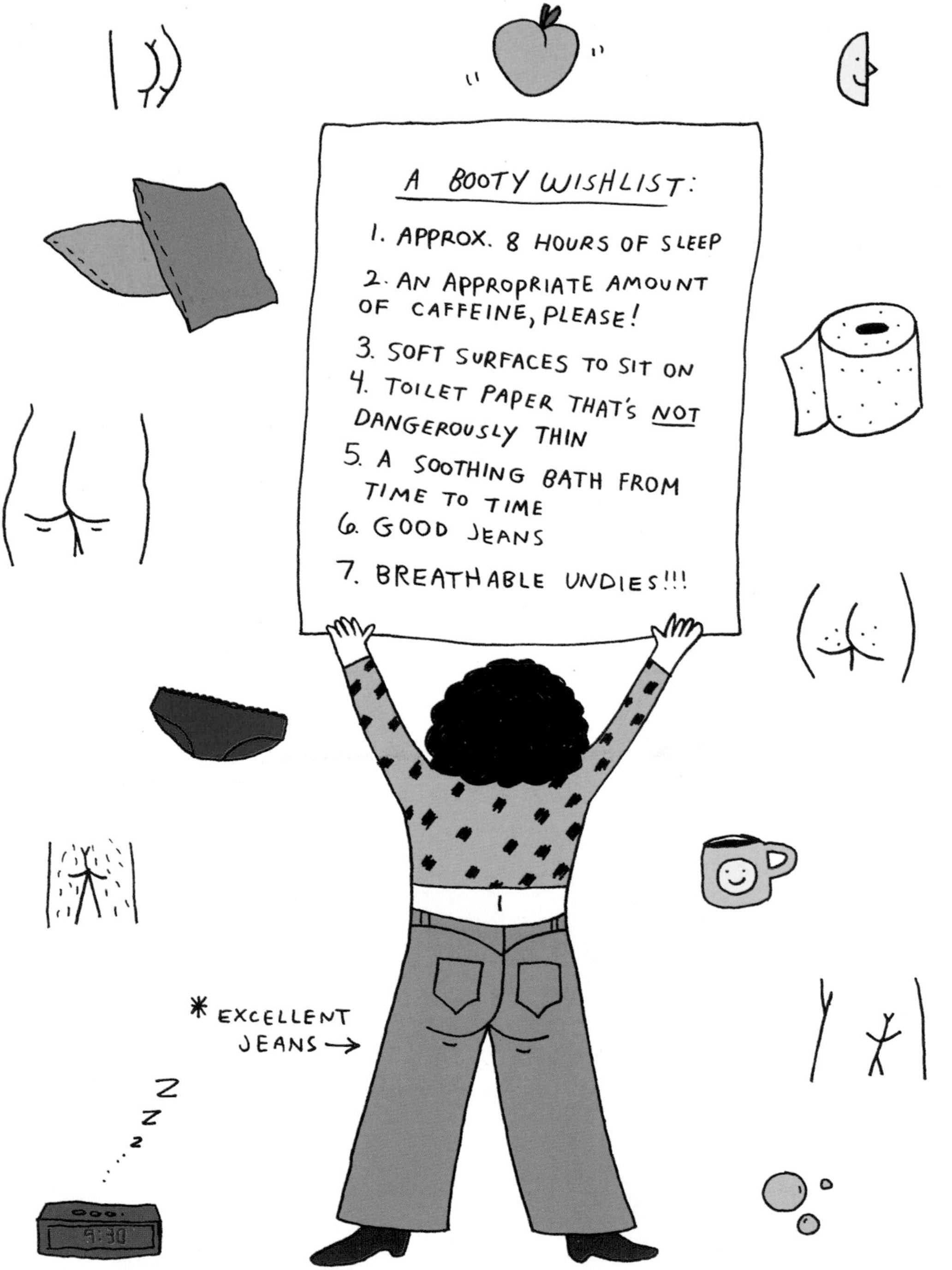
A BOOTY WISHLIST:
1. APPROX. 8 HOURS OF SLEEP
2. AN APPROPRIATE AMOUNT OF CAFFEINE, PLEASE!
3. SOFT SURFACES TO SIT ON
4. TOILET PAPER THAT'S NOT DANGEROUSLY THIN
5. A SOOTHING BATH FROM TIME TO TIME
6. GOOD JEANS
7. BREATHABLE UNDIES!!!
* EXCELLENT JEANS →
Z
Z
z
5:30

DON'T FORGET

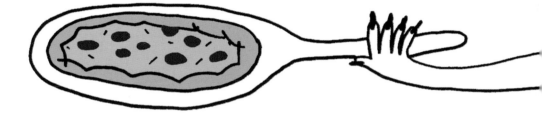

TASTY PIZZA

AN ADVENTURE FROM
TIME TO TIME

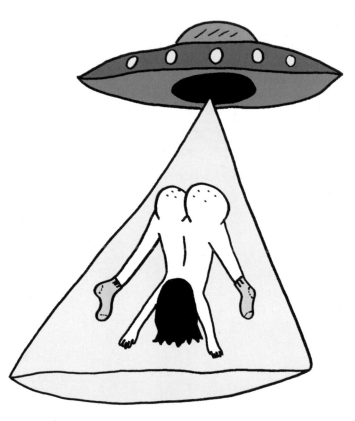

AND...

A DEEP
STRETCH

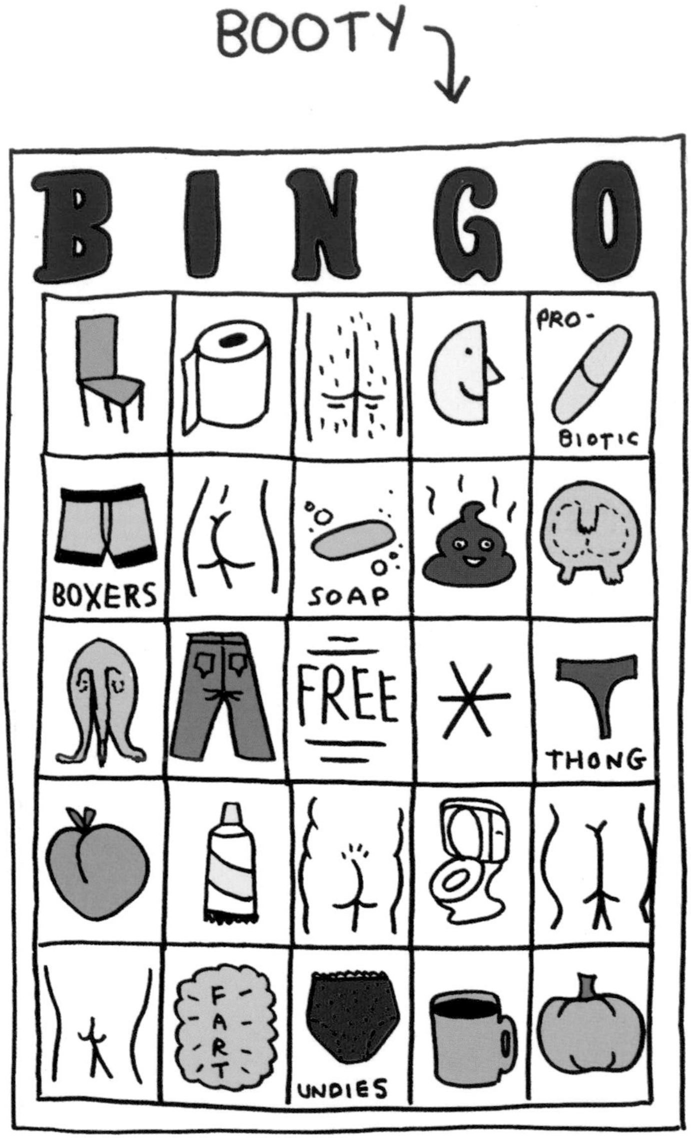
BOOTY
BINGO
PRO-
BIOTIC
BOXERS
SOAP
FREE
THONG
FART
UNDIES

A MOMENT
IN NATURE

BOOTY AFFIRMATIONS

Now that you've made it this far, it's time to talk fanny gratitude. That's right, offering appreciation for your butt can be a life-changer. From here on out, take a moment each day to thank your tushie. Read aloud and repeat:

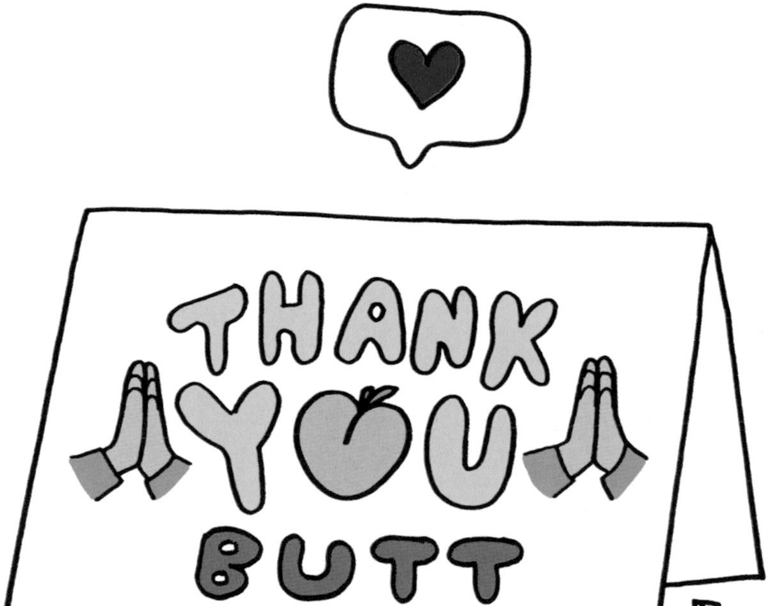
THANK YOU BUTT
HEARTFELT MESSAGE TO MY REAR END

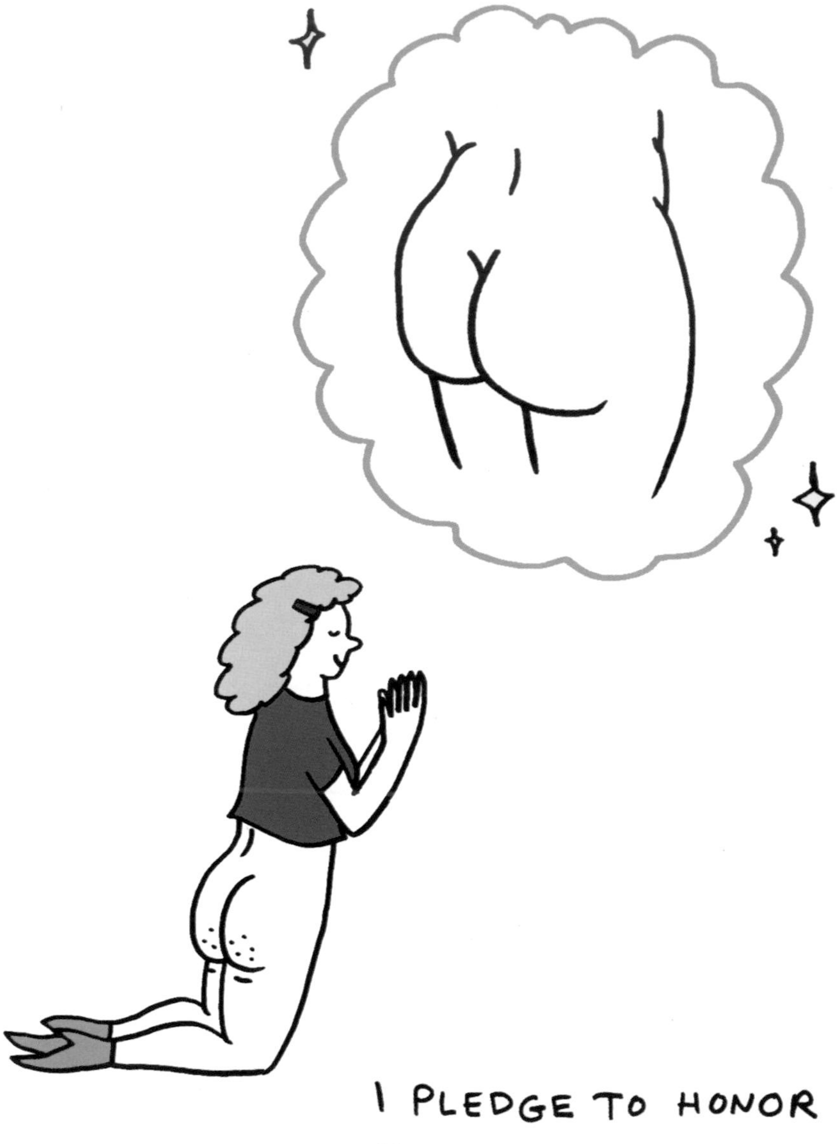

I PLEDGE TO HONOR YOU, DIVINE TUSH.

WATCH OUT FOR
SPICY FOODS!

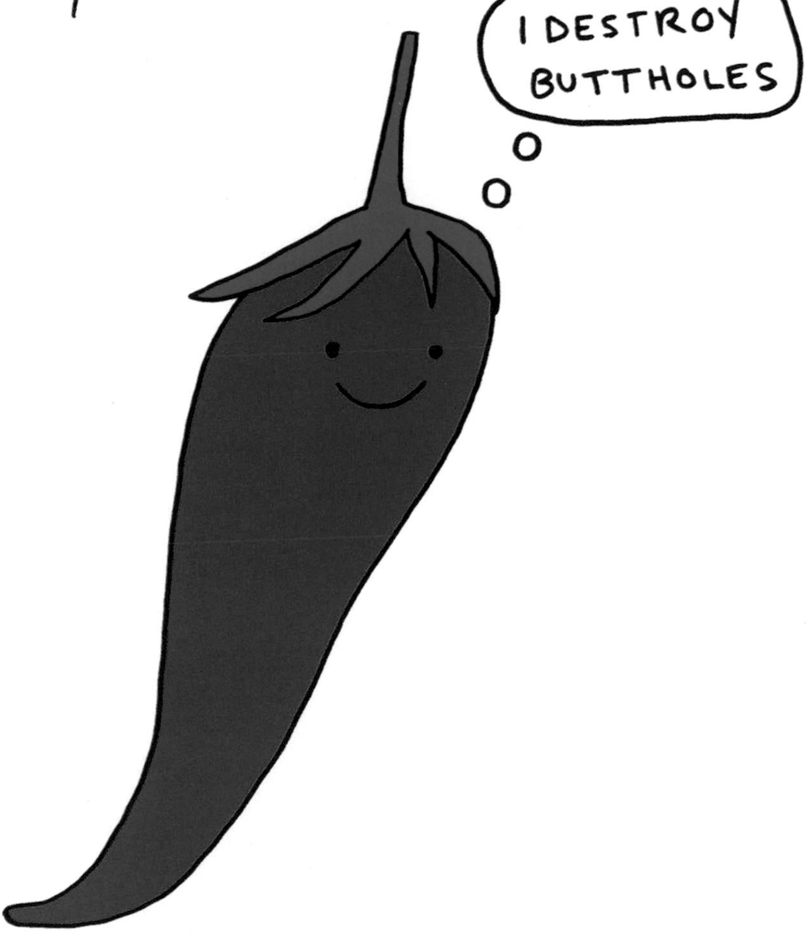
I DESTROY BUTTHOLES

*I VOW TO KEEP MY BUTT
CLEAN, COMFORTABLE, AND SAFE!

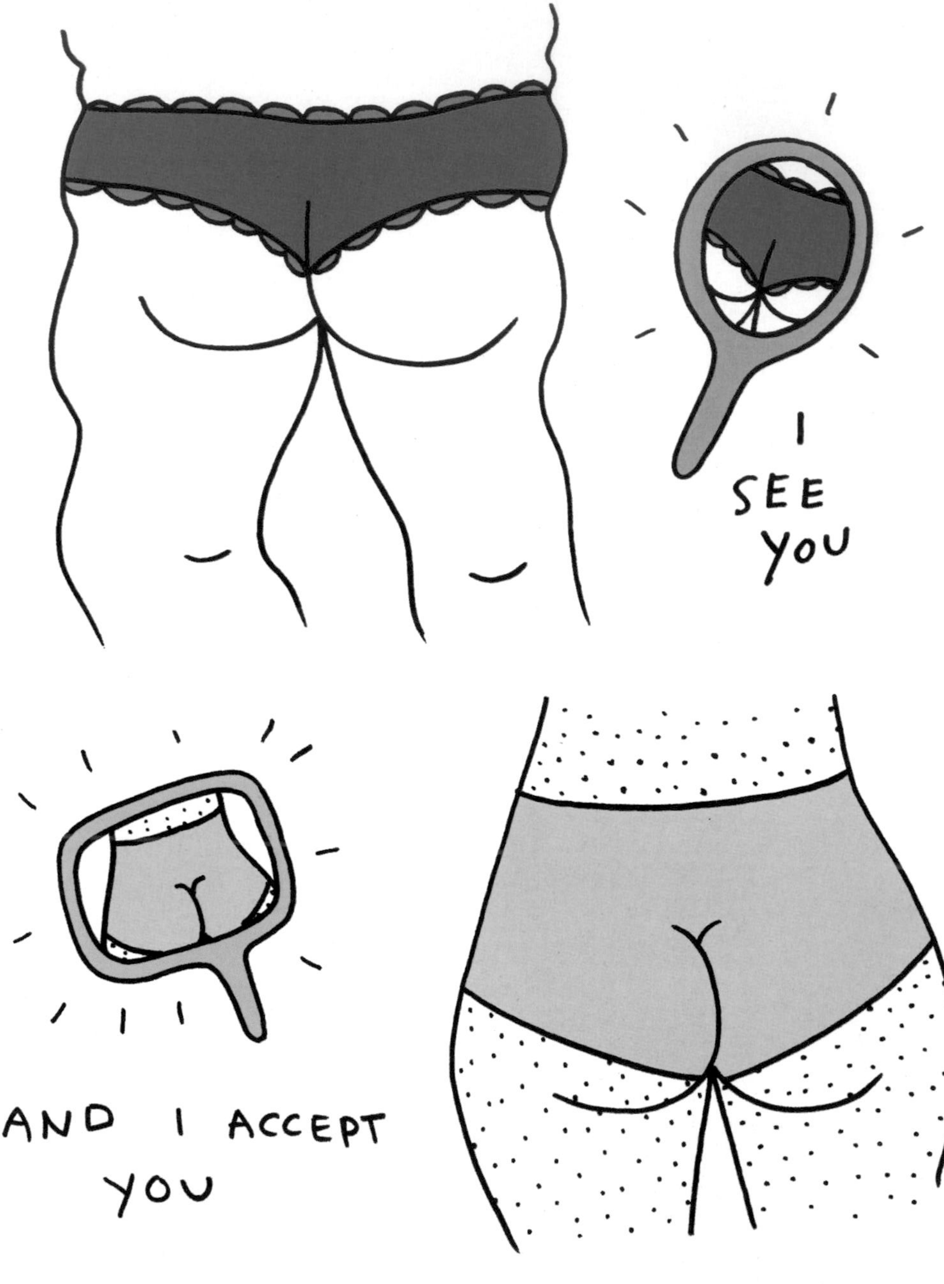
I SEE YOU
AND I ACCEPT YOU

MY ASS IS

Witchy

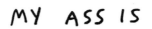

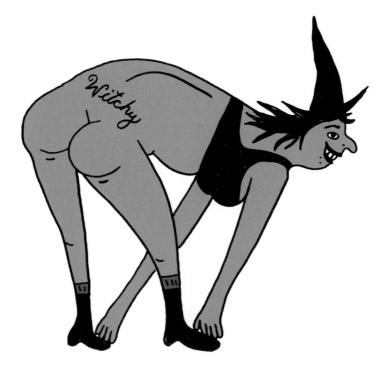

SUPERNATURAL!

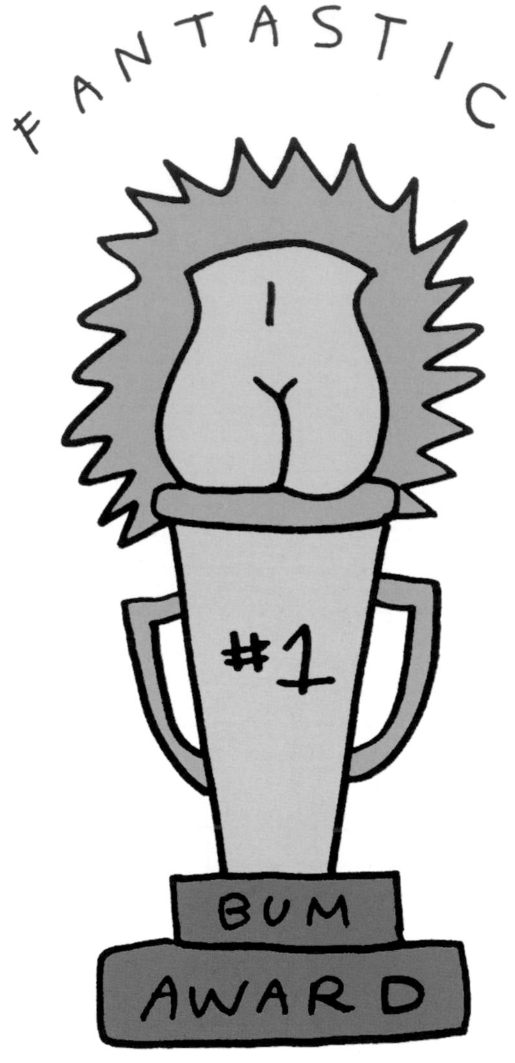
FANTASTIC
#1
BUM
AWARD

BECAUSE YOUR TUCHUS DESERVES IT!

MY BUTT IS

DRAW
YOUR
BUNS →
HERE

_____

↰
WHAT WORD BEST DESCRIBES IT?
      ∧
     KIND

THE END

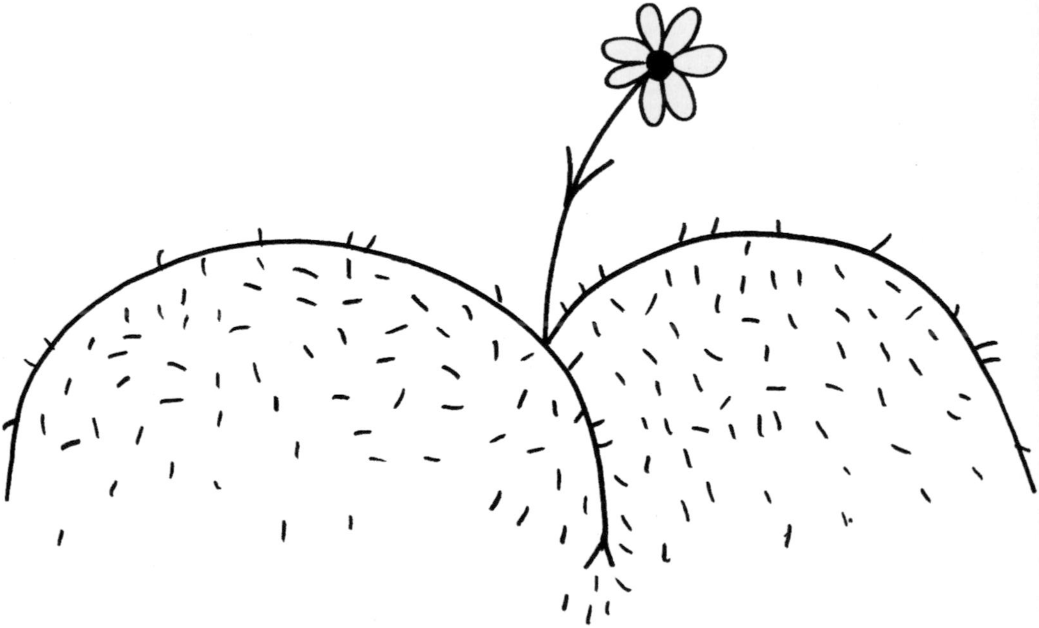

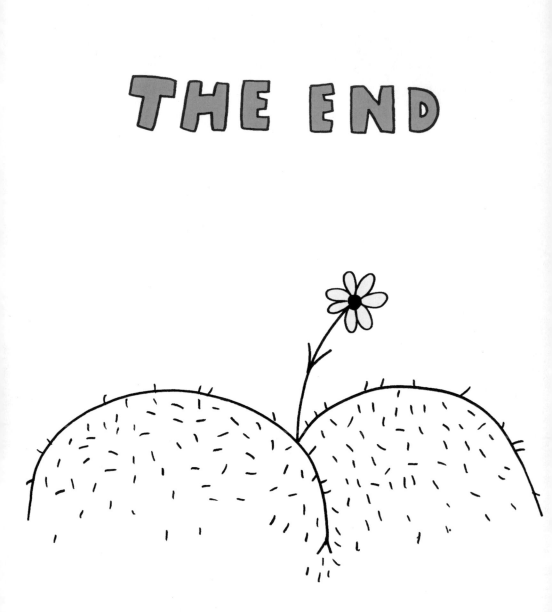

ACKNOWLEDGMENTS

I want to thank the wise old lady who came up to my booth at an art market and said to me, "You look innocent but you're quite raunchy." I've never felt so seen.

To my family and friends: You've put up with many years of butt-related art and your support has never wavered. Thank you for your endless love and fart jokes.

To each and every person who has supported my work, whether purchasing a custom portrait or following me on social media or attending one of my drawing workshops: you are wonderful and very appreciated.

ABOUT THE AUTHOR

〜〜 ☆ ▽ ᕦ ☮ ♡

Rachal Duggan is an illustrator based in Milwaukee, Wisconsin. Originally from the Chicagoland area, Rachal attended art school and worked in Chicago as an artist for over a decade. Best known for her highly coveted booty portraits, Rachal travels far and wide for pop-up events where she draws people on the spot. When she's not creating custom portraits or drawing her illustrated period story series, Rachal teaches virtual and in-person drawing workshops for all skill levels. Some of her clients include *The Guardian*, *NYLON* magazine, *Chicago Reader*, and the University of Wisconsin-Madison. See more of her work online at www.radillustrates.com.

RAD

THIS IS MY BUTT